Three Sons

Living for Christ in a Christian Family

PAUL SCHWANKE

First published by Paul Schwanke,
an Independent Baptist evangelist from Phoenix, Arizona.
Evangelist Schwanke is committed to preaching
and providing materials to assist pastors and churches
in the fulfillment of the Great Commission.

Evangelist Paul Schwanke
www.preachthebible.com

Cover design by Mr. Rick Lopez
www.outreachstudio.com

Special thanks to:
Pastor Ken Brooks
Calvary Independent Baptist Church
West Redding, Connecticut

ISBN-13: 978-1519693945
ISBN-10: 151969394X

Printed in the United States of America

CONTENTS

The Front Two Rows

YEARS AGO, I had the opportunity to speak with a youth pastor who was being used of God to build a successful ministry. When I say successful, I do not mean that it was a particularly large youth ministry. He wasn't invited to speak at great conferences. There was nothing 'cutting edge' about their activities. Most of the 'church growth' gurus wouldn't give the church a second glance.

But the work was very successful in the eyes of God. Men and ladies who grew up in the church are now making a difference for Christ. Some of the men are pastors. Some are missionaries. Some of the ladies are married to preachers. Others are busy in 'secular' work, yet they are faithfully serving the Lord. The product of the ministry is a host of people proving "what *is* that good, and acceptable, and perfect, will of God" (Romans 12:2).

I asked him how he did it, and I will never forget his response. "Everything changed when I stopped preaching to the back three rows and starting preaching to the front two rows."

It seems that most youth ministries are geared to the back rows-to the people that are not interested in the Bible. We want them to like church and the Bible. We want them to change their attitude toward God and their parents. So we give them the music they want; the activities they want; the fun and games they want. They graduate from high school and go on to ignore God and His word. They get all the attention but do nothing for Christ.

All the while, sitting on the front two rows, are kids that want to live for Christ. They love the Bible. They love their parents. They love their church. They want to do right. They don't need to be tricked into loving the Lord because they already do.

So this book is for that crowd. Let's encourage them to keep on pressing "toward the mark for the prize of the high calling of God in Christ Jesus" (Philippians 3:14). Let's encourage them to keep on "abounding in the work of the Lord" (1 Corinthians 15:58). Let's encourage them to "be found faithful" (1 Corinthians 4:2).

This book is for 'the front two rows'.

Chapter One

IT ALL CAME DOWN to one word, and what a word it was! Japheth, the oldest son of Noah, had never known a day in his life that the massive ark was not the main topic of conversation. He was now a 'young' 100 years old, and he could hardly believe his ears. His younger brothers, Shem and Ham, joined him in trying to understand what it all meant. They heard it. Their dad heard it. The word was given. We read it in Genesis 7:1.

"Come."

The last 120 years of their father's life was consumed by the command of God. The countdown began with these words: "My spirit shall not always strive with man, for that he also *is* flesh: yet his days shall be an hundred and twenty years" (Genesis 6:3). The clock had finally run down to zero, and it was time.

"Come."

It is fascinating that God did not point at the ark and tell them to "Go." Instead, He used the word "come." He was saying to them, "I know that you have doubts and worries about this ark, but you need to understand that I am asking you to come to me. When you walk into the ark, you will be in a safe place. I am here. No harm will come to you. If you want to be saved, come to me."

God would use that word many more times in the Bible. As he invited Noah and his family to "come" into the boat of salvation, so He invites any sinner to come to Christ and be saved. One of the most beautiful offers goes like this: "And the Spirit and the bride say, Come. And let him that heareth say, Come. And let him that is athirst come. And whosoever will, let him take the water of life freely" (Revelation 22:17). Another time, Jesus said it like this: "Come unto me, all *ye* that labour and are heavy laden, and I will give you rest" (Matthew 11:28).

It is a beautiful word. It is a beautiful invitation. But the word means there is a choice to make. Japheth, Shem, and Ham looked at the ark and saw the only way to escape the flood. They watched their father trust the Word of God and accept the promise of God. Now it was time for them to make their own choice. God said, "Come." What would they do? What would you have done?

Chapter Two

IN PROVERBS 13:15, the Bible says, "the way of transgressors *is* hard." Every night, we are reminded on the evening news that sin brings a hard life. It is hard to grow up in a family where the father or mother is a drunkard. It is hard to grow up in a family where there is violence. It is hard to grow up in a family where there is no money because someone is throwing it away at a casino. Even though Satan is a master at making sin look attractive, when it finally runs its course, there is always a hard price to pay. It is tough to live in a wicked home.

It is also difficult to grow up in a Christian family. To be sure, it is nothing like a home torn apart by booze or drugs or beatings, yet the great enemy makes sure it is not easy. When parents choose to live for God, without knowing it, they are inviting the attacks of Satan against everyone in their home.

So it was for Japheth, Shem, and Ham. Their father, Noah, had made a choice. The Bible says he chose to "walk with God" (Genesis 6:8). Here we are, nearly 5000 years later, and we applaud Noah. We know him as the man who saved the world. He may be a hero now, but that is not how they saw him back then.

Isn't it amazing that in our day Hollywood will make a movie about a holy man who lived 5000 years ago? Do they make movies and TV shows about righteous people living today? Do they show Christian families and Bible preachers in a good light, or do they make fun of them?

Noah lived in a time when "the wickedness of man *was* great in the earth, and *that* every imagination of the thoughts of his heart *was* only evil continually" (Genesis 6:5). They were not only doing wicked acts, but, in their thinking, they were constantly creating new ways to sin against God. They were dirty on the outside and on the inside.

A few years ago, an insurance company whose logo featured a red umbrella ran a TV commercial. It was a dreary, gray day. The rain was falling. There were hundreds of people with black umbrellas and black raincoats walking the same way down a busy city street. Suddenly, someone in a bright red raincoat, holding a bright red umbrella, was seen walking against the crowd. The insurance company was saying, "Everybody else goes the same way, but we are willing to be different. We want to go against the flow."

That's what Noah was like. The whole world was wicked. The whole world had turned against God. "But Noah found grace in the eyes of the LORD" (Genesis 6:8). It would seem that he was the only man in the entire world who wanted to please God.

Would you like Noah to be your father? We cry out, "Of course we would." But do you know what that would mean for you? It would mean that you would hear your father criticized everywhere. It would mean that you would be made fun of. Your entire family, you included, would be crazy to the normal world.

It is not easy to have a father who wants to please God. It means there are TV shows and movies that everyone else watches that you won't see. It means there is music they love that you don't listen to. It means there are games they play that you don't play. It means there are kids that will laugh and make fun of the way you act, the way you dress, the way you talk, the way you wear your hair, and the way you live. It means that your family will be different from just about every other family in your neighborhood.

It took a lot of courage to stand against the world like Noah did. Today, it takes a lot of courage to be a Christian teenager in the middle of what God calls a "crooked and perverse nation" (Philippians 2:15). If it was easy to be righteous, then everyone would do it!

Chapter Three

I AM ALWAYS AMAZED when people look at little babies and say they look like family members. "He has Uncle Billy's nose! She has her mother's ears!" I hardly ever see the similarities. To me a baby looks like himself. It has to be a really obvious trait before I see any resemblance.

A child may 'get' his parents eyes or ears or nose, but there are other traits he learns without genes. Some kids learn how to lose their temper by watching their parents. Some learn how to swear. Some learn how to drink booze. Some learn how to smoke. Some learn how to gamble. Some learn how to cheat. Some learn how to lie. It is easy to pick up bad habits.

But a son or daughter can also pick up good habits. They can learn how to laugh; how to show respect; how to work hard; how to sacrifice for others; how to tell the truth. These lessons, along with many others, combine to form a person's character.

Japheth, Shem, and Ham learned some great things from their father. Noah taught them how to build. He taught them how to work with animals. He taught them how to endure in difficult times. But for all the virtues he taught his sons, the greatest thing he taught them is found in Genesis 6:8: "But Noah found grace in the eyes of the LORD." He taught them how to go to Heaven.

These simple words describe the greatest lesson parents can teach their son or daughter. He taught them that the only way to Heaven was by the grace of God. Sinners will never be good enough to impress God. They will never pay their way to Heaven or work their way to Heaven. The only way to be saved is by the wonderful grace of God, and Noah taught his boys that you must 'find' grace, not 'earn' it. We find grace at the Cross of Christ.

Noah also taught his sons how to walk with God (Genesis 6:9). Noah did not run ahead of God, nor did he take a stroll with Him, but every day he consistently and patiently walked with God. It is the key to being a good Christian. We start walking and keep on walking with God.

Noah taught them the importance of obeying God. "Thus did Noah; according to all that God commanded him, so did he" (Genesis 6:22). His heart was to please God and follow his commands. It wasn't just the order to build the ark. Noah wanted to obey God in **all** areas of life.

What a testimony Noah was. Patiently and consistently, he taught Japheth, Shem, and Ham how to go to Heaven, how to walk with God, and how to please God. His sons had a dad that was different from every other dad in the world.

Are you thankful for your mom and dad? Have you ever thanked the Lord that He gave you parents who are trying to teach you how to please God? Have you ever thanked your parents for showing you how to be saved?

The next time you see a news story of some teenager committing a horrific crime, it would be a good time to bow your head and thank God that He put you in a family that taught you differently. Then it would be a good time to raise your head and thank your 'Noah.'

Chapter Four

ON FEBRUARY 11, 1962, Parade Magazine published the following brief account:

At the village church in Kalonovka, Russia, attendance at Sunday school picked up after the priest started handing out candy to the peasant children. One of the most faithful was a pugnacious lad who recited his Scriptures with proper piety, pocketed his reward, then fled into the fields to munch on it.

The priest took a liking to the boy, and persuaded him to attend church school. This was preferable to doing household chores from which his devout parents excused him. By offering other inducements, the priest managed to teach the boy the four Gospels. In fact, he won a special prize for learning all four by heart and reciting them nonstop in church. Now, 60 years later, he still likes to recite Scriptures, but in a context that would horrify the old priest. For the prize pupil, who memorized so much of the Bible, is Nikita Khrushchev, the former Communist czar.[1]

Nikita Khrushchev was an evil man. In the 1930's he was a main part of the 'Great Purge' in Russia, a time when political leaders imprisoned and executed millions. He became the leader of the godless communist government in Russia. One day, when one of their cosmonauts (we call them astronauts) said he could not find God, Khrushchev foolishly said it proved that God did not exist. He was a great enemy of freedom.[2]

It is one thing to learn the Bible to get a candy bar, but it is something else to learn the Bible because we love God. It is not hard to bribe someone to act like a Christian on the outside, but it is impossible to compel someone to be right with God in their heart.

In studying the Bible, I have learned to admire and respect an Old Testament prophet named Ezekiel. God wanted him not only to preach his messages to the people, but also to show His word to them. Ezekiel was required to do some pretty strange things. Like Noah, he was not a popular man.

Once, God told him to shave his head, which in his day, was a very disgraceful thing to do. Then God told him to divide his hair into three piles. Next, he was told to burn one pile, slice the second pile with a knife, and scatter the third pile into the wind. On another occasion, God told him to lie on his side in public next to a model of an enemy attacking Jerusalem. He did it for 430 days in a row! Yet another time, God told him to gather some strange ingredients to make a loaf of bread. When it was time to bake the bread, God told him to use human waste for the fire. Needless to say, the people had a lot of things to say about Ezekiel, but he was simply obeying God.

The people in Ezekiel's day had sinned against God, yet they convinced themselves they were right with God. They thought that they were exempt from any punishment because they belonged to the nation of Israel. They would say, "After all, we are the people of God. Our greatest city is Jerusalem. God has always protected us. He will never judge us!"

They were making a dangerous mistake. They assumed all was well because of their heritage. Their spiritual fathers were men like Abraham and Isaac and Jacob and Joseph and Moses and Samuel and David. Their history was full of mighty prophets like Elijah and Elisha and Isaiah and Jeremiah. They thought, "God has invested too much in our nation. He will never allow an enemy to conquer us!"

So God told Ezekiel to preach these words: "Though these three men, Noah, Daniel, and Job, were in it, they should deliver *but* their own souls by their righteousness, saith the Lord GOD" (Ezekiel 14:14). A few verses later, he added these words: "Though Noah, Daniel, and Job, *were* in it, *as* I live, saith the Lord GOD, they shall deliver neither son nor daughter; they shall *but* deliver their own souls by their righteousness" (Ezekiel 14:20).

Noah, Daniel, and Job were wonderful men of God. In the grand history of the Bible, they distinguished themselves. Noah built the ark when the world was evil. Daniel was tossed into the den of lions because he was a man of prayer. When the whole world seemed to be crushing Job, he would not curse God. These three men were special.

By their right actions, these men honored God and pleased Him, yet the Bible says their righteousness was not enough to save their own children. They were not able to be 'righteous' for anyone else. Righteousness is a personal choice between an individual and God.

Japheth, Shem, and Ham had a wonderful father. He was righteous when everyone else was wicked. When God told him to build an ark, he responded in obedience. In 2 Peter 2:5, Noah is even called a "preacher of righteousness." There have been very few humans who were as righteous as he.

But God said that Noah was not righteous enough to save his boys. He was not righteous enough to make his sons clean before God. No parent can ever do that. If a son or daughter will be right with God, it will be the result of choices that son or daughter has made. No one can be right with God for someone else.

Often, when parents are saved at a later age, they have great regrets about their life before they were saved. They can remember their teenage years when they committed sins they cannot take back. It is true that God forgives all sin, but sometimes there are scars and memories of those sins that never go away.

Now these parents have trusted Christ. They know the guilt and the pain of past sins, and even though the blood of Christ has cleansed them, there are results that haunt them. Because they love their children, they want to do everything humanly possible to make sure their kids never experience sin as they did.

That is a noble thing. That is a godly thing. No parent who loves the Lord would ever want their own child to make a mess of his life. They want to do everything possible to protect those they love. Because they love the Lord, they never want to hurt Him again, and they want to make sure their family won't break His heart.

Occasionally good parents make an honest mistake that comes out of their love for the Lord. They try to be righteous for their kids. They make the error of thinking, "Because my children are following my ways, then everything is okay in their hearts."

They can't do that. Noah couldn't be righteous enough for Japheth, Shem, and Ham. No parent can be righteous for his children.

If you will be right before God, it will be the choice you make in your heart. No parent, no matter how much they love their children, can force them to be righteous sons or daughters. Candy bars can't do it. Parents can't do it. Only you can make that choice.

Chapter Five

WHEN NOAH WAS 480 years old, God told him, "My spirit shall not always strive with man, for that he also *is* flesh: yet his days shall be an hundred and twenty years" (Genesis 6:3). I know it is amazing to think of people living for more than 900 years in those days, but God said it was so.[3]

So the countdown begins. God had already told Noah that there was great wickedness throughout the world. The "men of renown" (Genesis 6:4) were military heroes that had become famous. It seemed they led others down an evil path, and before long the world was out of control. Enough was enough, and God announced that judgment would come in 120 years. "I will destroy man whom I have created from the face of the earth; both man, and beast, and the creeping thing, and the fowls of the air; for it repenteth me that I have made them" (Genesis 6:7). Noah would be saved by building an ark.

Imagine Noah thinking about that project! He knew the vain, sinful people in his world would never help with such a work. They were living in wickedness "continually" and had no desire to obey God. How many times he must have said to his wife, "I don't know how I am going to do it all by myself. This ark is so large, I need some help! How am I going to do it?"

I suppose that Noah and his wife assumed they would never have any children. All their relatives were having kids when they were much younger, and when he celebrated his 480th birthday, he must have figured it would never happen for them. Later in the book of Genesis, Sarah, the wife of Abraham, laughed at the notion she would get pregnant. "Shall I of a surety bear a child, which am old?" (Genesis 18:13). I wonder if Mrs. Noah said the same thing!

In Genesis 5, the Bible gives us a number of family histories. The fathers seemed to start having children when they were about 100 or so. Some a little earlier, and some a little later, but 100 seemed to be an average age for them to start having children.

Noah had a calling from God, but he needed help. At the age of 480, he started preaching messages of coming judgment and warning people to repent of their sins. That message went nowhere, so Noah began to gather materials he would use for the ark. Then God told him that the ark would be 300 cubits by 50 cubits by 30 cubits (450 feet long; 75 feet wide; 45 feet high). What a massive job!

"Lord, I need help!"

God gave him the help he needed. When he was 499, his wife got pregnant. Soon, Japheth was born (Genesis 10:21). Shem was born two years later, and he was quickly followed by Ham (Genesis 9:24). At just the right time, God gave him a family. His sons would be strong enough to build the ark. They would be young enough so they could repopulate the earth after the flood. It was just the right boys at just the right time! Japheth, Shem, and Ham were put in Noah's family because God had a purpose for them. God not only had a special plan for Noah, He had his perfect will for his sons as well.

Have you ever wondered why God put you in your family? Why did He give you to Christian parents? Why didn't He put you in a lost family? We often think of the will of God in terms of what adults do, but God has His plan for every Christian.

I have met some wonderful missionary children all around the world. Some of these families live in very undesirable places. I have been in places where the word 'poor' doesn't describe what it is really like. Villages are dangerous and dirty, and sometimes the smell nearly knocks a person out. But there are the missionary families serving God. These 'MK's' (missionary kids) are incredible people!

I spend a lot of time with pastors and their families. I don't know if there is a harder thing in the world for a young person than being a 'PK' (preacher's kid). They are often criticized because they are not as 'perfect' as somebody thinks they should be. They have to sacrifice time with their mom and dad. They live in a fishbowl where everyone is watching. I admire PK's!

If God has put you in a Christian family by His will, then you have a great opportunity to serve Him. Perhaps He thought so much of you that He gave you a preacher for a dad. Perhaps He trusted you so much He put you in a distant mission field because He knows you are strong enough to make it. Perhaps you mom or dad is serving the Lord in a church, and you can be a blessing helping in a Sunday School class or a bus route.

You can serve God just like your parents. You can bring people to Christ. You can honor the Lord. You can live for the Will of God, so that one day He will say to you, "Well done, good and faithful servant."

He did not make a mistake by putting you in your family.

Chapter Six

MANY YEARS AGO, my father played in a baseball game in Connecticut. It was quite a special game because of one of the players on the other team. You may have heard of him. His name was Babe Ruth. I have a picture of my dad and his teammates posing with Babe Ruth. It is a special photo to me.

My sons enjoyed listening to their grandfather tell the story of the day he played against Babe Ruth. Grandfathers are good at telling stories. There is something very special about a grandson or granddaughter hanging on to every word. Many great life lessons can be learned from Grandpa's stories.

Japheth, Shem, and Ham had a grandfather named Lamech. When the boys met their granddaddy for a hamburger and fries, they must have asked him for a story. Lamech did not play baseball against Babe Ruth, but there was a very famous person he knew.

His great, great, great, great, great, great grandfather was Adam. When Lamech was born, Adam still had 238 years to live.

Can you imagine the conversation? "Boys, Adam told me what it was like in the Garden of Eden. He told me how Satan came in the form of the serpent and tricked great, great, great, great, great, great grandma Eve. That dirty snake! I hate 'em. He told me about his own choice to disobey God. He tried to cover his sin but that did not work. Soon God expelled him from the Garden of Eden, and this world has never been the same."

No doubt, Grandpa Lamech told the boys stories about his own grandfather. "My grandpa was quite a man! There was no one like him! One day, when my father was born, he decided that he was going to live for the Lord. He reminded me a lot of your dad. He was a prophet of the Lord. When he preached, he was always warning people to get ready to meet God. He told them that one day the Lord was coming with ten thousands of his saints."

"My grandfather started walking with God and he never stopped. And do you know what happened? One day God just took him to Heaven. He never died! He loved to preach that the Lord was coming, and one day, He came and took grandpa Enoch to Heaven!"

The boys would also visit their great grandfather. "Great grandpa, why do you have such a funny name?"

The old man must have laughed. "So you think Methuselah is a funny name? Well, let me tell you, it is a very important name. My father, Enoch, was always preaching about prophecy and events in the future. When I was born, God told him what to name me. My name means, 'When he dies, it shall come.' I am the son of a prophecy preacher, and my entire life is a prophecy."

"Boys, one day God is going to judge the sins of the wicked. Everywhere we look Satan and his forces seem to be winning. The wickedness is great in the earth. It is easy to think that God is ignoring humans, but one day I will die. That is the day the judgment comes."

It seemed that Methuselah would live forever. The Bible says that he lived for 969 years, longer than any other human life recorded in the Bible. I can hear one of the sons of Noah ask their great grandfather why he lived so long.

"Grace! The reason I am still alive is because God wants sinners to be saved. I am a walking time bomb of the coming judgment of God. The reason He has allowed me to live so long is to remind people that he loves sinners and has patiently extended the invitation for them to come! But boys, I am getting up there. When you hear that I have died, you will know it is time to get into the ark."

Then one day the message came. Methuselah was dead. Noah and his sons knew it was time to escape the wrath of God. Their granddaddy had told them.

There are a lot a great things to learn from your grandparents. A wise grandson or granddaughter knows how to listen.

Chapter Seven

"AND THE LORD said unto Noah, Come thou and all thy house into the ark" (Genesis 7:1). The invitation was not just for Noah, it was for his entire family.

A wise preacher once said, "God has many children, but He has no grandchildren." He meant that multitudes of people have believed on the Lord Jesus, trusted Him as their Savior, and are now the "sons of God" (John 1:12). But no one can ever be saved through another human. No one is saved because his or her parents are saved. There is no such thing as group salvation or family salvation.

This is the picture of Genesis 7. The Lord invited the entire family of Noah to come into the ark and be rescued from the coming flood. The offer was there, but each person had to act on it.

Notice how the Bible tells us they responded:

"**And** Noah went in, **and** his sons, **and** his wife, **and** his sons' wives with him, into the ark, because of the waters of the flood" (Genesis 7:7).

"In the selfsame day entered Noah, **and** Shem, **and** Ham, **and** Japheth, the sons of Noah, **and** Noah's wife, **and** the three wives of his sons with them, into the ark" (Genesis 7:13).

An English teacher would look at those verses and notice that the word "and" is found nine times. Normally, we don't think much of the word 'and,' but when it is found that many times in such a short space, there is reason to pay attention. In fact, when so many conjunctions are found in a small sample of writing, the English teachers have a word for it. It is called a 'polysyndeton.'

When a 'polysyndeton' is found in a Bible verse, it is God's way of getting us to pay attention. When we read a list, it is easy to slide through the names and miss the message, but by repeating the word 'and,' the Bible is stopping us and reminding us to look. God is saying, "Don't miss a name. Don't lump them together. There is an important message in these lists."

It was quite the day. The animals were safely on board. There were seven of the clean animals on board. Clean animals could be eaten and used in sacrifices to God. There were two of the unclean animals-one male and one female. Now it was time for humans to join them.

The first invitation was extended to Noah. Notice that Noah was not saved by his righteousness. Noah was saved by the grace and mercy of God. His willingness to obey God and be a righteous man made him different from everyone else in the world. So God tells him, "Noah, come." And Noah walked through the door into the ark.

This is where the polysyndeton matters. The three sons watched their dad walk into the ark, and though their father trusted the Salvation of God, that would not be enough for the boys to be saved. The judgment of flood would soon come, the offer of God's Salvation was right in front of them, but they had to make their own choice. One by one, each of the boys decided to trust God's provision. One by one, they followed their father into the ark.

"**And** Shem, **and** Ham, **and** Japheth." God tells us to stop and watch each one of these sons. Their dad was saved, but that did not mean they were saved. God invited them to come, but they still had a choice to make.

So we watch Shem. What will he do?

"I am deciding to obey God. I am deciding to trust His salvation."

And Shem walks through the door into the ark.

Now we watch Ham. His father is saved. His brother is saved. But he has his own personal choice to make. Soon we watch him walk through the door into the ark. Ham has made his decision.

But what about Japheth? His father trusted God's offer. His brothers did as well. But Japheth will die with the rest of the world if he does not make the right choice. He decides to trust the Lord. He enters into the ark.

It works the same way for their three wives. The verse reads: "the three wives of his sons with them." One would think it would say: "the wives of his sons." The wording is unique because God is also drawing attention to the fact that these women had a choice to make. Just as the sons were not saved because their father was saved, these ladies were not saved because their husbands were saved.

"**And** Shem, **and** Ham, **and** Japheth." Even with a father like Noah, these three boys had to make their own decision. As much as a father wants to see his child saved, he cannot make it happen. No one goes to Heaven unless they personally "believe on the Lord Jesus Christ" (Acts 16:31).

You will never be saved by the choice of someone else. It is a huge mistake to assume that you are a Christian because you live in a Christian family. Salvation is a personal choice that only you can make.

It may be that your father and your mother and your grandfather and your grandmother and your brother and your sister and your uncle and your aunt and your cousin and your neighbor and your best friend and your workmate and your schoolmate and a lot of other people you know are saved. But you better make sure there is an *'and me'* in that list!

Chapter Eight

"AND SHEM, AND HAM, AND JAPHETH." Did you notice something surprising about that list?

Japheth was the oldest son, but he was not the first one to board the ark. In our society, we may not think too much about that. However, in the days of the Bible, there was usually a proper order. The leadership of the family would be given to the oldest son when the father died. He would be given more honor and a better inheritance than anyone else. There were great responsibilities and great blessings for the oldest son.

But now it was time to get on the ark, and the second son, Shem, goes first. The respectful thing would have been to give preference to the oldest brother, but Shem steps out. He did not wait for his oldest brother to lead the way.

When we read the Bible, for obvious reasons, God only gives us a quick part of the story. If every biography and every story were completely explained, the Bible would be so large we could never carry it. The Apostle John said that if all the things that Jesus did were written down, he supposed "the world itself could not contain the books" (John 21:25). So we only get a part of the story.

That is one reason I am looking forward to Heaven. We will have forever to get all the details of the magnificent stories in the Bible. Imagine how glorious it will be to hear Jesus teach the Bible!

Perhaps we will see videos of Bible events. If so, I would like to see how Genesis 7 played out. The animals were safe on board, and now God invited the humans to "come." I would like to see the camera focus on Shem. Perhaps he looked at his brother to see if he would go. Maybe Japheth was wondering what to do. Maybe he was a little afraid. Maybe he wondered if the pitch on the outside of the ark would keep them dry.

I can see him step around his brother with an 'excuse me.' He was not going to wait around to see what Japheth would decide. He was going to be on that ark when the door was shut even if no one else in the world joined him. Next came the youngest son Ham. Japheth, the oldest, was last.

At the end of the preaching service, we give an invitation for people to be saved. I always ask that people respectfully bow in prayer as we encourage the sinner to trust the Lord. Then we invite people to come, so that we might open the Bible and lead them to Christ. This is a serious moment in a service.

One of the things that amazes me is watching how people respond to the invitation to be saved. So often, people will look around to see what others are going to do. They may be under conviction of sin, and they may know that they need to be saved, but they have to see what their friend is going to do.

Years ago, a man of God was preaching about Hell. He noticed some teenagers in the back of the auditorium laughing during the message. There is nothing funny about Hell.

May I stop and encourage you to get up to the front of the auditorium? There is nothing more spiritual about sitting in the front, but three decades of preaching has taught me that the further people sit to the back of the auditorium, the harder it is to get their attention. When people are talking, laughing, texting, or passing notes, they bother others. Sit where there are the fewest distractions.

The teenagers were not only bothering others, they were disturbing the preacher as well. Finally, he looked at them and said these words: "Your friends my laugh you into Hell; but they will never laugh you out of Hell."

The old preacher was right. You may follow your friends into Hell. You may follow their steps, their attitude, their sin, and you might say "no" to Christ right along with them. You may follow their steps into

Hell, but that is where it will end. There is no 'exit sign' in Hell. It is forever.

Shem would tell us, "I was not going to miss that invitation for anybody or anyone! If my brother wasn't going to go, it didn't matter. God did not have to ask me twice!"

So it is true for us today. Every important decision that we make for the Lord, from being saved to serving Him, is an individual choice. We cannot afford to wait for someone else or let them decide for us.

"I am getting on that ark!"

Chapter Nine

"THE LORD shut him in" (Genesis 7:16).

What an wonderful statement! Noah had been working on the ark for 120 years. Some of that time was given to preaching a message of coming judgment. Some of that time was given to gathering the needed materials. Some of that time was given to the construction of the ark. Some of that time was given to organizing the animals God brought to the boat.

It is interesting to see that God gave an extra "seven days" (Genesis 7:10). Great Grandpa Methuselah had died, and the custom of the day called for a seven day period of mourning for the dead. Jewish teachers claim that God held the rains so that Noah and his sons could give an appropriate burial for the righteous man. Another teacher thinks the seven days were God's grief for the world's rejection of His Salvation.

One thing is certain. God kept the offer to be saved open for seven more days. The message inviting people to "come" was a patient one indeed.

But the last invitation had run its course. With the family of Noah safe inside, it was time for God to act. His mighty Hand shut the door of the ark.

That door teaches some great lessons. First, there was only one door. God told them, "A window shalt thou make to the ark, and in a cubit shalt thou finish it above; and **the door** of the ark shalt thou set in the side thereof" (Genesis 6:16). The fire marshall may not have approved of an ark with only one entrance and exit, but that is what God commanded. There was one door to enter. There was one door to shut.

In much the same way, Jesus is the only door to Heaven. He said, "I am the door: by me if any man enter in, he shall be saved" (John 10:9). You will notice that He did not say, "I am *a door*." He is the *one and only door* to eternal life. John 14:6 is very familiar: "Jesus saith unto him, I am the way, the truth, and the life: no man cometh unto the Father, but by me."

There is another wonderful lesson here. Notice that God did all the work. God did not ask Noah to get his sons to pull the door closed. He did not ask them to throw the lock. God took care of the door.

The only thing Noah did was obey God's commands. One of the most amazing things about these chapters in Genesis is the fact that Noah never speaks. The first time he is actually quoted is in chapter nine.

If a person will be saved from Hell and receive eternal life, he must understand that God does all the work. He sent His son to die on the Cross. He offers the gift of eternal life. He washes our sins away. He does it all. Our responsibility is to believe and obey. "For by grace are ye saved through faith; and that not of yourselves: *it is* the gift of God: Not of works, lest any man should boast" (Ephesians 2:8-9).

An eight year old boy approached his pastor one day wanting to be baptized. The pastor had some concerns as to whether the young man truly understood salvation, so he asked him to explain it. The boy said, "That's easy. I did my part and Jesus did His part."

That response worried the pastor. Knowing that the Bible repeatedly says that Salvation is "not of works," the pastor asked him, "What do you mean when you say that you did your part, and Jesus did His part?"

The fellow responded, "I did all the sinnin'. Jesus did all the savin'."

The little guy had it right. When it comes to going to Heaven, Jesus does all the work.

There is another great lesson from God's shutting the door. With that single act, the destinies of every human on the earth were settled. For Noah and his family, the shutting of the door meant that they were secure in God's Salvation. For the rest of the world, it meant they were forever excluded. They had rejected the call of God, and now they would die in their sins.

The Bible says, "He that believeth on the Son hath everlasting life: and he that believeth not the Son shall not see life; but the wrath of God abideth on him" (John 3:36). The verse is powerful because of its simplicity. A person who has Christ as his Savior possesses everlasting life. He cannot lose it. It cannot be taken away. It is something he 'has.' But the man without Christ does not have eternal life. Instead, the wrath of God, (the judgment of God), is presently abiding upon him. For the Christian, eternal life does not begin when he dies; it is something he possess es right now. For the unsaved person, the judgment of God is already upon him.

God shut the door. People were either in the ark or out of the ark. It was one or the other.

God saves sinners. People are either saved by Christ, or they are unsaved and without Christ. It is one or the other.

If you have never believed on the Lord Jesus Christ as your Savior, I challenge you to read Romans chapter 5 where the offer of Salvation is given so clearly. I encourage you to obey the command of the Word of God: "Believe on the Lord Jesus Christ, and thou shalt be saved" (Acts 16:31).

There came a moment in time when God shut the door, and the invitation was no longer available to the people of Noah's day. For the same reason, God said, "Behold, now *is* the accepted time; behold, now *is* the day of salvation" (2 Corinthians 6:2). I plead with you to be certain you have accepted God's invitation.

Chapter Ten

YEARS AGO, I was sitting in the home of a detective who worked in the city of Chicago. He was responsible for investigating crimes inflicted upon young children. I could hardly believe some of the case files and photos that he was showing me. I did not think it possible that humans could ever do such horrible things to young boys and girls.

I remember preaching with a missionary in Manila. One night, after a wonderful service, we went to the home of a church member to eat a fabulous meal. When we finally made our way back to the missionary's house, it was about 11:00 pm.

I noticed the streets were filled with young children, both boys and girls, who couldn't have been more than nine or ten years old. There were gangs of them everywhere. They would steal anything and everything.

My missionary friend explained that most of these kids had no home. They wandered the streets aimlessly. Most of them would either die in their teenage years, wind up in jail, or in the case of the girls, even worse. I couldn't help but think, "These kids should be tucked into a safe bed somewhere." It was tragic. Parents who should have been protecting their children didn't care.

It has been estimated that there may be 100 million such 'street children' in the world. I don't know if that is an accurate number, but my many travels to distant lands convince me that there is a great number of boys and girls that no one cares for. In the eyes of the world, they are not worth saving.

If you were to ask most people what Noah was famous for, they would answer, "The man built an ark." Everyone believes that. But if you were able to ask Noah what he was doing, he would give a different answer. To find his response, we would need to go to the book of Hebrews in the New Testament. It is amazing that God allowed 2,500 years to pass before He gave us these words:

"By faith Noah, being warned of God of things not seen as yet, moved with fear, prepared an ark to the saving of his house; by the which he condemned the world, and became heir of the righteousness which is by faith" (Hebrews 11:7).

Noah did not build the ark so that he might become famous. Noah did not build the ark so that Sunday School teachers would have a lesson. Noah did not build the ark so that they would make a movie about his life.

Noah built the ark to save his house (his family). That was his motivation! When he was tired and his body ached with pains, (and you can be sure a man 550 years old had his share of aches and pains), there was a purpose that got him out of bed each morning. He woke up every day with these words ringing in his mind: "I've got to save my family! I've got to save my family! I've got to save my family!"

We might imagine someone walking by and looking at this monstrous boat. It was, after all, 450 feet long (a football field is 300 feet long.) A man might stare at the ark for a while, and then see Noah working at the top of the ark, almost five stores high. We can hear him holler, "Hey Noah! What are you doing up there? Building a boat?"

Noah would yell back at the man: "No! I am not building a boat!"

"Then what are you doing up there?"

"I am saving my family!"

We know that it was 120 years from the time God told Noah that judgment was coming until the ark was finished. What we don't know is the incredible amount of money it must have cost Noah to build the ark. To save his family, Noah consumed an immense amount of time, money, and energy, but it was worth it.

"I have to save my family."

It costs a lot of money to pay for a week of camp. It costs a lot of money to put a child in a Christian school. It takes an incredible amount of energy to teach a child at home. I have witnessed parents who make amazing sacrifices to keep their children away from influences that can ruin their lives, because they want to save their family.

Have you ever thanked your mom and dad for the sacrifices they make to protect you? According the US Department of Agriculture, it now costs the average family $245,000 to rear a child for 18 years. This does not even include the cost of a college education![4]

Think of that number. It is almost 1/4 of a million dollars per child! Your mom and dad have given for you in ways that you will never know. When they were saving money for something special, you needed braces. When they wanted to get away for a special trip, you had music lessons. When they were tired, you had a ballgame.

If you have parents who care enough to save their family, you have something wonderful indeed.

Just ask those kids in Chicago and Manila.

Chapter Eleven

WHY DIDN'T THE PEOPLE get into the ark? The reason might surprise you.

Jesus put it like this:

"But as the days of Noe were, so shall also the coming of the Son of man be. For as in the days that were before the flood they were eating and drinking, marrying and giving in marriage, until the day that Noe entered into the ark, And knew not until the flood came, and took them all away; so shall also the coming of the Son of man be" (Matthew 24:37-39).

I am sure there were many reasons the people refused to enter the ark. I suspect many doubted; many laughed; many mocked. But Jesus said there was another reason. People did not go into the ark because they were too busy!

Some were eating and drinking. Others were planning and attending weddings. Ultimately, they did not enter the ark because they had too many other things going on. They were too busy to take care of the most important matter in their life and family.

Your pastor has probably invited thousands of people to come to church. A few, but most likely not too many, have laughed in his face. Most people say something else.

"I know I need to come, but I am too busy this week."

"Pastor, I am so busy at work. We are working overtime."

"I would be there on Sunday, but we are going to a family reunion."

The excuses go on and on. People know they should make time for God, but it really isn't a priority. Church? Not when my favorite football team is playing. Not when there is a golf game to be played. Not when it rains. Not when the weather is nice. Like the people in Noah's day, folks are a little too busy to consider spiritual things.

As an evangelist, I do a lot of traveling. I have spent more nights in hotel rooms than I could care to count, and I have noticed a trend. Years ago, hotels were pretty quiet and deserted places on weekends. The business travelers had all gone home. There were times when I was the only guy in the hotel.

Not any more! Hotels are packed on weekends, but it is not the traveling businessman. It is now young people on sports teams. When I leave a hotel on Sunday morning wearing a tie and jacket and a Bible under my arm, I am surrounded by people wearing baseball and softball uniforms, soccer jerseys, and basketball warmups. Just as I am going to my church, they are going to their house of worship.

When I preach in the Far East, I find a different issue on the weekend. Very few young people will go to church because they are studying seven days a week. Monday through Friday finds them in school; Saturday and Sunday finds them with a tutor. They are consumed by the idea of getting into college. Grades are more important than God.

I often wonder if their parents ever consider eternity. They may go home at the end of a weekend with a trophy, but what about the day they stand before God? They may graduate with honors, but at the end of a life, SAT scores are not as important as one might think.

That, however, is not your story. You are in church Sunday School, Sunday morning, Sunday night, Wednesday night, Revival Meetings, Prayer Meetings, Bible Conferences, and Missions Conferences. You go to Summer Camp, School Camp, Winter Camp, and Youth Meetings. Some even attend Christian Schools. There are 365 days a year, and you might be in church for 300 of those days. It is conceivable that someone growing up in a Christian home may hear as many as 8000 sermons!

That is a lot of Bible. That is a lot of opportunity to make choices that please God. That is a great gift, but such a gift has a warning: "For unto whomsoever much is given, of him shall be much required" (Luke 12:48).

God has invested in you. He has given you Christian parents. He has given you His Word. He has given you an understanding of spiritual things. He has given you a family where His will is more important than the world's wishes. You are living in a family that is not too busy for God.

Are you giving Him a return on the investment?

Chapter Twelve

MY DAD, who is now in Heaven, was a great father, but he was a lousy barber. I went to elementary school in the 1960's, a very rebellious time in American history. It was a time of riots and trouble. It was a time of loud and crass music. It was a time when patriotism was laughed at.

And it was a time of long hair. Today, people don't seem to get so worked up about hair, but in the sixties, it was a big issue. Long hair was the sign of a rebel.

My Dad was not a big fan of long hair, so he decided to give his sons haircuts. He never went to barber college. Instead, he practiced on us. I don't think he ever really learned how to do it.

There are many different styles of haircuts, but my Dad only knew one style. Short. When he was finished, it pretty much looked like he put a bowl on the top of our heads and cut off everything else. At least, that is what all the kids at school said when they were laughing at me. Actually, if my Dad could have waited 40 years, our haircuts would have looked really cool. But in the 1960's, let's just say our haircuts made us look really different.

My Dad cut our hair because he didn't want us to look like rebels. More importantly, he taught us the Bible every day so we wouldn't grow up to be rebels. I would have to admit that I did not like people laughing at me. I would have to admit that I did not appreciate that I was different from everybody else. It wasn't always easy.

I would also guess that a lot of the kids at school were glad they didn't have the kind of father I had. Their dads didn't have rules. Their dads let them dress like they wanted. Their dads didn't care what time they came home. When they saw my haircut, I suspect many of them said, "I am glad that his father is not my father."

Years later, when I was a senior in high school, I still had shorter hair than everyone else. When my classmates were out partying on Friday nights, I was at our church's Bible study. I never drank with them; rocked out with them; did drugs with them. By this time, I had no desire to live such a lifestyle, because I had long since surrendered my life to the will of God. And I still had a dad that would not let me engage in those activities.

They were still laughing at me. "You don't go to parties. You don't go to dances. You don't go to movies. You don't go to the prom. You don't drink. What do you do for fun?" They really laughed when I told them I went to Bible Study for fun. I suppose they said, "I am glad that his father is not my father."

Somehow, I managed to play on our high school baseball team. My Dad found a way to come to almost every game. Many of my teammates had watched their parents get a divorce, and they didn't have a father who cared to come to the games. Another told me that his father drank so much he was glad that he didn't come and embarrass him. Some dads were too busy with work to come. So most of the time, it was my Dad up in the stands all by himself.

He learned the names of everyone on the team. When they came to bat, he would cheer for them like they were his own sons. He made them laugh. He supported them.

One day, after a game, we were on the bus heading back to the school. The conversation got around to my dad. I explained what it was like having a Christian dad who loved the Bible. We talked about living in a family where a father cared enough to have rules. Then one of my friends said, "I wish I had a dad like that."

It must have been tough being Japheth, Shem, and Ham. When your father is building a boat 1 1/2 times the size of a football field, people are going to notice. This was not a fishing skiff or a little rowboat; it was a monstrosity. As he worked on the project for 120 years, you can be sure people were talking.

If they made fun of me for having a dad who gave me a funny haircut, I can imagine what they said to Noah's sons. I suspect there were times when it was not fun being the son of Noah.

When Noah preached against the wickedness in the land, I suppose there were a lot of kids that said, "I am glad that he is not my father!"

When everyone else was living for the fun that sin could bring them, I am sure there were a lot of kids that looked at Noah and said, "I am glad that he is not my father!"

When everyone else gave themselves to finding satisfaction, and Noah gave himself to finding grace in the eyes of the Lord, I suppose most of Japheth, Shem, and Ham's friends said, "I am glad that he is not my father!"

When everyone else walked in sin, and Noah walked with God, you can be sure they said, "I am glad that he is not my father!"

When everyone else did what they felt like doing, and Noah did according to all that God commanded him, I am quite certain they said, "I am glad that he is not my father!"

Then one day: "In the six hundredth year of Noah's life, in the second month, the seventeenth day of the month, the same day were all the fountains of the great deep broken up, and the windows of heaven were opened. And the rain was upon the earth forty days and forty nights" (Genesis 7:11-12). It was terrifying. "And every living substance was destroyed which was upon the face of the ground, both man, and cattle, and the creeping things, and the fowl of the heaven; and they were destroyed from the earth: and Noah only remained *alive*, and they that *were* with him in the ark" (Genesis 7:23).

As the waves of water carried people to a horrible death, do you know the last thing the friends of Japheth, Ham, and Shem thought?

"I wish I had a dad like that."

Chapter Thirteen

"AND GOD REMEMBERED NOAH, and every living thing, and all the cattle that *was* with him in the ark" (Genesis 8:1). Obviously, God never forgot about Noah, Japheth, Shem, Ham, and the ladies. When the Bible tells us that God "remembers," it is a way of explaining how God goes about keeping His promises. In Genesis 6:18, God made this promise: "But with thee will I establish my covenant; and thou shalt come into the ark, thou, and thy sons, and thy wife, and thy sons' wives with thee." Then in verse 19, God promised to "keep *them* alive."

It must have been quite a time in the ark. Their daily chores meant they had to feed and water the animals and clean up after them.[5] The supernatural events certainly had their attention. When the "windows of heaven were opened" (Genesis 7:11), the torrential rains "overflowed" the earth (2 Peter 3:6). At the same time, "the fountains of the great deep (were) broken up." Water began to gush uncontrollably from wells and springs beneath the ocean.

Most Creation geologists believe that the opening of "the fountains of the great deep" refers to the breakup of the earth's crust into plates. The subsequent rapid, catastrophic movement of these plates would have released huge quantities of hot subterranean waters and molten rock into the ocean. As the hot water gushed through the fractured seafloor, the water flashed into superheated steam and shot high into the atmosphere as supersonic steam jets, carrying sea water that eventually fell as rain.[6]

It is likely the flood began with a massive tsunami that circled the earth with incredible speed. There would have been volcanoes, mudflows, and ecological upheaval like the world has never seen since. I can only imagine what Japheth, Shem, and Ham must have experienced at that time.

I expect they must have been happy to be alive, but there is something depressing about 40 days and 40 nights of rain. Scientists call it seasonal affective disorder (SAD). When people don't get enough sunshine, they become distressed, tired, and prone to eat too much.[7] I wonder how well the brothers got along?

When God dried the earth, He did so with a special wind. It would not be hard to imagine the size of the waves that were stirred by that wind. I can almost hear the ark groaning as it is tossed to and fro. Someone who has spent the night riding out a hurricane may be able to relate to Noah and his family, but this 'hurricane' did not last for one night. It went on for 150 days.

When the days are added together, the boys were on the ark for a solid year. Since they were human like us, it is easy to envision their hardships and their fears. There must have been occasions where they wondered if they would ever put their feet on dry ground. I would not be surprised if they wondered if God may have forgotten about them.

But God "remembered" them. Of course He did. God always remembers His promises and His people. He always keeps His word.

Not long ago, I was preaching at a church in Arizona. A pastor walked up to me and introduced himself. He told me that we had met many years earlier at a camp in California. Nearly 30 years had passed, but I still remembered preaching that week. He told me this story:

"One night, you were preaching on the importance of the Bible. You encouraged us to promise God that we would make a habit of reading and studying the Bible. That night, I came forward during the invitation and promised God that I would have a personal time of Bible study every day. From that day until today, there has only been one day that I did not take time to read the Bible (almost 30 years later). That was the single greatest decision I have made in my Christian life; it is the greatest reason I am now a pastor."

There is a reason for that. When we read the Bible, study the Bible, memorize the Bible, and meditate over the Bible, the result is a faith that grows (Romans 10:17). It is not a sudden spurt. It is usually hard to recognize. But a daily walk in the Word of God will slowly produce an assurance that God will keep His promises. We don't see it happening, but we are becoming strong in faith.

The problem is not whether God will keep His Word. The issue is whether you and I have the faith to believe Him. That faith develops as we build Bible habits in our life.

A pastor once visited an old man suffering from painful rheumatism and found him with his Bible open in front of him. The minister noticed that the word "proved" was written repeatedly in the margin. He turned over a few pages and found, "God is our refuge and strength, a very present help in trouble." "Proved." Next to John 1:12 he had written "Proved." He had received Christ by believing and had indeed become a child of God. He had proved that promise of God's Word. Verse after verse had been proven in the old man's life.

It is one of the great reasons to begin your own personal study of the Bible. I would encourage you to make a daily journal of the lessons you learn from

God's Word. The more we read the Bible, the more we see God proving Himself again and again. One day, you will find yourself trusting the Lord with the greatest decisions of life. Your Bible will become your friend and guide.

When your heart begins to doubt, your Bible will remind you that God remembers.

Chapter Fourteen

WHAT A GREAT MAN Noah was! He is remembered in the Bible as a "just" and "perfect" man who "walked with God" (Genesis 6:9). His obedience is a great example for all of us. He didn't argue with God. He simply did what God commanded him. No wonder we still honor him for his remarkable faith (Hebrews 11:7).

When Noah left the ark, God was ready for him. First, the Bible says that "God blessed Noah." Then, God made this promise: "And I, behold, I establish my covenant with you" (Genesis 9:1,8).

The blessing of God and the promise of God. What a gift was given to Noah!

A blessing in the Bible normally meant that a greater authority would bestow a benefit on someone who was less in stature. A king might bless the people. A father might bless the son. But there is no blessing to compare with the thought of Almighty God smiling upon a human and giving him His gift.

God blessed Noah with the command to "be fruitful, and multiply, and replenish the earth." Despite the great judgment that God had sent to the earth, He was not done with humans. They had flaunted their sins before God, but He was ready to give mankind a second chance. That is a great story of mercy. That is a great blessing.

Next, God "established" His covenant. The word "established" sent a strong message. God was saying, "Noah, you have my word on it. My promise will not fail. It will stand as long as time shall be." God promised Noah that He would never again destroy the earth with a flood.

We as humans do not always keep our word. But "God *is* not a man, that he should lie; neither the son of man, that he should repent: hath he said, and shall he not do *it*? or hath he spoken, and shall he not make it good?" (Numbers 23:19) There is nothing safer than trusting in the very promise and guarantee of God. When God gave His word that He would never destroy the earth with a flood, it was "established" for eternity.

The blessing of God and the promise of God. If you have grown up in a Christian family, you have no doubt witnessed the blessing of God upon your parents. Perhaps there was a financial or medical need that God provided for them. Maybe you have seen God answer their prayers. God has blessed them.

If you have a mom and dad who love the Bible and make family decisions based on the Word of God, you have seen God honor His Word time and time again. Unsaved families are often torn apart by confusion that results from parents who don't know where to stand, but there is a stability that is found in a family where Mom and Dad study the Bible, know the Bible, believe the Bible, and practice the Bible. Make sure you do not take your parents for granted.

But there is something else to notice in Genesis 9. God did not simply bless Noah; He "blessed Noah and his sons." God did not make His promise with Noah alone; He said, "I establish my covenant with you, and with your seed after you."

We know that God blessed Noah and gave His word to Noah, but the same verses tell us that the blessings of God and the promises of God were for His sons! God was not just the God of Noah. He was the God of Japheth, Shem, and Ham. They enjoyed the blessings just like their dad. They could say, "The Word of God is not only for our dad; it is for us!"

If you have parents that have known the blessings of God and the Word of God, then you are privileged! But those blessings and promises are for you too. You can walk with God and see Him meet your needs. You can say: "My God shall supply all (my) need" (Philippians 4:19). You can know that "every word of God *is* pure" (Proverbs 30:5). You can build your life claiming the very same promises in the Bible that your parents have followed.

George Hatch raised a large family of seven boys and five girls in the sand-hills of northwestern Nebraska. One Sunday morning, a neighbor rushed over to help the Hatches get the freshly mown hay into the barn. Clouds were rolling up in the West, and it was quite apparent that a rainstorm coming.

"Let's get your hay up before the storm hits!" exclaimed the neighbor.

"Thank you for your kind offer," said Mr. Hatch, "but this is Sunday, and I am going to take my family to church."

"But you'll lose your hay," pleaded the neighbor.

Yet the Hatches went to church, and while they were sitting in the service, the rainstorm spoiled the hay.

"See, I told you that you would lose your hay," said the neighbor.

"Yes," replied Mr. Hatch, "I lost my hay, but I saved my family." It is doubtful that the neighbor fully understood.

George Hatch did save his family. Today, down into the third and fourth generations, grandchildren and great-grandchildren are serving the Lord. His children realized that the very God that daddy loved and served was the same God they could follow. [8]

Your life will forever change when you genuinely believe that God is not simply the God of your parents or your pastor. You can say, "O LORD my God, in thee do I put my trust" (Psalm 7:1). He is not just their

God; He is my God! The Bible is not just their book; it is my book!

Chapter Fifteen

I WISH this chapter were not in the book.

To be honest, if I were the author of the Bible, Genesis 9:18-27 would not be there. But I am not the author of the Bible. God is. And the reason these verses are in the Bible is that God is not afraid to remind us that the greatest of human men are still human. They are going to make a mess of things.

We often put heroes of the Bible on a pedestal, but God reminds us that the mightiest of His servants were still men of "like passions as we are" (James 5:17). They had times of doubts and fears and troubles. They had occasions where they failed the Lord, and sometimes they failed miserably (see the stories of David and Peter).

Noah made a mess.

Preachers have a difficult time with this story. There is a lot of guessing and speculation as to what exactly happened, but I have learned it is always best to let the Bible say what God wanted it to say. It is wrong to add to the Bible. It is wrong to take away from the Bible. God told us exactly what we need to know.

Here is what happened:

"And Noah began to be an husbandman, and he planted a vineyard: And he drank of the wine, and was drunken; and he was uncovered within his tent. And Ham, the father of Canaan, saw the nakedness of his father, and told his two brethren without. And Shem and Japheth took a garment, and laid it upon both their shoulders, and went backward, and covered the nakedness of their father; and their faces were backward, and they saw not their father's nakedness. And Noah awoke from his wine, and knew what his younger son had done unto him." (Genesis 9:20-24)

A husbandman is a 'man of the earth'-a farmer. Noah planted a vineyard, and when the grapes were harvested, he drank of the wine from the grapes. He drank so much that he became drunk.

Some people rush to the defense of Noah and claim that he did not understand what he was doing. But the Bible tells us in Matthew 24:38 that people were eating and drinking before the flood. I am afraid that Noah knew that a man who drinks booze will get drunk.

Drunks do a lot of foolish things. The Bible says that Noah was "uncovered within his tent." We know from the words that Noah undressed himself, passed out, and was lying naked in his tent. Worse, the flap of the tent was open, and others could see him.

There are many reasons why God says a Christian should not even look at booze (Proverbs 23:31). Liquor, nakedness, and moral sins all go together. When a man is looking for a woman to satisfy his lusts, he usually does not look for her in a church service on Sunday. He goes to a dimly lit bar or dance hall on Saturday night. When the booze flows, people lose their standards and their sense of right and wrong. Booze dulls their conscience.

Booze never made a man a good daddy. Booze never gave peace to a worried woman. Booze never gave a teenager a future. Booze never made a strong marriage. No one has ever come to the end of their life and wish they had drunk more, but countless millions have come to the end regretting they ever took the first drink.

Booze has destroyed countless families. Drunks regularly beat their wives and children. Earlier, I mentioned the detective who investigated horrific stories of child abuse in Chicago. One day, I asked him, "How many cases of abuse did you investigate where booze or drugs were *not* a contributing factor?"

He shot back: "Never! Never!"

Broken lives, broken families, and broken futures are the product of liquor. Noah could not handle the booze. You are making a grave mistake if you think you can. If you promise God that you will never drink and you keep that promise, one day you will be glad that you did. You will never find yourself saying, "If I could do it again; I think I would have drunk booze."

So a drunken Noah is lying naked in his tent with the flap open. What happens next is shameful. Ham "saw the nakedness of his father," and went out and "told his two brethren." That part of the story is clear, but the confusing statement is found in verse 24. "Noah awoke from his wine, and knew what his younger son had done unto him."

Some people assume that Ham committed a dirty act against his father, but the Bible does not say that.[9] What it does say is that Ham saw his father and told his brothers about it. Ham could have chosen to look the other way and not say a word, but instead he chose to disgrace his father. There is shame in nakedness, and there is a reason that God repeatedly tells His people to dress appropriately and modestly.

The Bible has a lot to say about sons and daughters showing honor and respect to their parents. One of the Ten Commandments says, "Honour thy father and thy mother: that thy days may be long upon the land which the LORD thy God giveth thee." In Romans 1 and 2 Timothy 3, the Word of God lists a number of sins that angers God. Some of these sins are of the most evil variety, and in both lists, God condemns children who do not obey their parents.

God expects obedience. God expects honor. When Ham saw the shame of his father, he proceeded to embarrass his dad. Notice how differently Japheth and Shem reacted. Instead of joining in Ham's mocking, they "took a garment, and laid *it* upon both their shoulders, and went backward, and covered the nakedness of their father; and their faces *were* backward, and they saw not their father's nakedness" (Genesis 9:23).

Japheth and Shem knew their dad's condition, and instead of laughing at him, they showed great respect. They covered their dad, and they did so in a manner that they never even looked at his nakedness. In the middle of a bad situation, they found a way to keep dignity and respect for Noah.

If you live in a family for eighteen years, you are going to see some embarrassing things. Just as you are not perfect, your parents are not perfect. Someone might get angry. Someone might say an unkind word. If Noah could lose it, we can lose it as well. A wise son or daughter knows how to act like Japheth and Shem. They know there is a time to look away; a time to keep someone they love from being embarrassed. Foolish sons or daughters gossips behind their parent's back. They laugh at their parent's problems. Their critical spirit will come back to haunt them one day.

I should emphasize another point here. Noah did something foolish, but he did not do something illegal. Sadly, we live in a society where adults have been guilty of evil crimes against children and teenagers. They get away with their crime because they tell vulnerable people not to tell anyone.

If a crime is committed, it is not time to be silent. "Honor thy father and mother" does not mean you allow someone to assault or abuse. The Bible says that God created governments to be a "terror...to the evil" and to "*execute* wrath upon him that doeth evil" (Romans 13:3-4). Jail or worse is the only place for an adult that attacks or molests. You are expected to defend yourself and protect others. God never wants you to hide criminal acts, even if they are committed by your relatives.

There is a difference between 'foolish' and 'illegal.' If you are not sure about that difference, have a private conversation with your pastor.

It is the wise young man and wise young lady who knows how to control his or her tongue. It is the wise one who will honor and respect his parents.

Chapter Sixteen

HAVE YOU EVER considered your legacy? If you have, you are a very unusual and wise person! Very few people plan beyond next weekend. To think about the generations to come is unheard of.

But everyone leaves a legacy. We will leave behind a testimony of right or wrong. We will leave behind a story that is good or bad. We will blaze a path that people will want to follow or reject.

Japheth, Shem, and Ham were no different. Centuries later, we can read an entire book and learn from their ways. In following the legacy of their dad, they show us great decisions that we can make in our lives. Ham showed us errors we can avoid.

When Ham saw his father in the tent, I am sure he never stopped to think what his actions would do to his grandchildren and the descendants that followed. His disrespect toward his father was serious, and when Noah woke up, he said, "Cursed *be* Canaan; a servant of servants shall he be unto his brethren" (Genesis 9:25). This is the first time in human history a man is recorded as giving a curse. Ham's family would not simply be servants and common workers; they would be the lowest of slaves. They would be the servants of sin.

Like many other chapters in the Old Testament, Genesis 10 traces family histories. When one studies the family of Ham, the nations of Egypt and Canaan stand out as his legacy.[10] Egypt would become famous for pagan religions and multiple gods. Canaan would become notorious for dirty sexual practices. Because they were so evil, God eventually made this law: "After the doings of the land of Egypt, wherein ye dwelt, shall ye not do: and after the doings of the land of Canaan, whither I bring you, shall ye not do: neither shall ye walk in their ordinances" (Leviticus 18:3). The sons of Ham certainly followed their daddy's example.

But there were other sons. After he cursed Ham, Noah said, "Blessed *be* the LORD God of Shem." It was Shem who stepped out first to get on the ark. Now, it is Shem that leads the way in honoring Dad. Because Shem loved and feared God, the blessing that Noah directed to God indirectly fell on him. The greatest blessing was the fact that the LORD was the "God of Shem." Shem did not have a religious relationship with God; he had a personal Savior.

It should come as no surprise to discover righteousness in the line of Shem. When reading Luke

3, which gives a long list of families (called genealogies), people often skip the last sixteen verses. But if you study it carefully, you would find that Shem had some rather famous descendants. They were named Abraham, Isaac, Jacob, (Joseph), and David. Two of his family tree laid a little baby in a manger in a little village called Bethlehem.

There is a big difference between the line of Ham and the line of Shem!

But what about Japheth? Noah promised, "God shall enlarge Japheth." His family went on to build the great empires of Greece and Rome. The Bible promised that Japheth would "dwell in the tents of Shem," a wonderful prophecy saying that Gentile people would join in the glory of Shem's spiritual blessing. God's Salvation would not be for the Jews alone; it would be for all nations.

As a young boy, I was fascinated by the ocean. It is an amazing thing to watch the rolling waves and feel the power of the water crashing at your feet. It still amazes me to visit a beach on the Pacific Ocean and imagine the land on the other side of the water. If I point in a certain direction, the land straight ahead is Australia. If I change my stance just a little, the land in front of me would be the Philippine Islands. A little more, and I might be facing Japan or China or South Korea. There is a long way between Sydney, Australia, and Beijing, China, but if you are starting that journey from a beach in California, it is only a matter of which way you turn your body. A slight change of direction makes a big difference as to where you arrive.

So it is with a legacy. It is the reason that you need to keep a tender heart to the Bible and the preaching of the Bible. It is why God said, "My son, hear the instruction of thy father, and forsake not the law of thy mother" (Proverbs 1:8). Little decisions you make today may not seem so significant, but they will add up to important life choices down the road. Your decisions determine your destiny.

The Year was 1620. As the Mayflower crossed the Atlantic, a ferocious storm arose. Wind and waves were beating the ship on every side. When a young passenger named John Howland came up on deck, the force of the storm swept him into the sea. It seemed he would perish for sure.

Somehow, he managed to grab a rope trailing from the ship and held on for dear life. Men on board pulled the rope while John rose with the waves until he was next to the boat. They fished him out with a boat hook, saving his young life. John Howland would live for many years.

Watching from the deck was a twelve year old girl named Elizabeth Tilley. Years later, she would marry John Howland, and they would be blessed with ten children, eighty-two grandchildren, and a multitude of descendants. Those descendants included three presidents: Franklin Roosevelt, and both of the George Bushes. [11]

Think about that story for a moment. One more wave and those three great Americans would never have existed. One event in 1620 is impacting lives nearly four centuries later!

It is important that you make the right choices. After all, you are not only choosing for yourself. You are making decisions that will effect your great, great, grandchildren! A wise man or lady will always consider tomorrow.

Chapter Seventeen

"CHOOSE YOU THIS DAY whom ye will serve" (Joshua 24:15). It is a privilege to have parents who love the Lord, but every son and daughter have their own decisions to make. Japheth, Shem, and Ham had the same Godly heritage, saw the same righteous example, heard the same wonderful invitation, and saw the same tender protection of God. Still, they had to make their own choices.

Our lives are the result of choices we make. Some may be small; some may be huge; yet the choices will determine the direction of our lives. We will choose the right direction or the wrong direction. We will choose the right spouse or the wrong spouse. We will choose to live for the here and now or eternity.

Most importantly, we will choose Heaven or Hell.

One day, Jesus gave a special warning to those who saw His mightiest works but did not repent:

"Woe unto thee, Chorazin! woe unto thee, Bethsaida! for if the mighty works, which were done in you, had been done in Tyre and Sidon, they would have repented long ago in sackcloth and ashes. But I say unto you, It shall be more tolerable for Tyre and Sidon at the day of judgment, than for you. And thou, Capernaum, which art exalted unto heaven, shalt be brought down to hell: for if the mighty works, which have been done in thee, had been done in Sodom, it would have remained until this day. But I say unto you, That it shall be more tolerable for the land of Sodom in the day of judgment, than for thee." (Matthew 11:21-24)

Hell is serious business. It is horrible when a thief, a drunk, or a murderer rejects Jesus and goes to Hell. But there is something worse about someone who has seen God work and is still not saved. He grows up in a family where God has delivered the home from the ravages of sin. He witnesses the mighty Hand of God in answering prayer. He feels the conviction of the Holy Spirit upon his life but rejects Him.

How many invitations can the Lord give? How patient can He be? It is dangerous to think that God will operate on your schedule. You cannot simply tell God when you are going to be saved and how your life will work. The Bible says, "Boast not thyself of to morrow; for thou knowest not what a day may bring forth" (Proverbs 27:1). "Behold, now *is* the accepted time; behold, now *is* the day of salvation" (2 Corinthians 6:2).

There are times when we need to examine ourselves to see if we are "in the faith" (2 Corinthians 13:5). The answers are found by searching the Bible and taking God at His word. When it comes to going to Heaven, you cannot have your parent's word on it; you cannot have your pastor's word on it; you cannot have a counselor's word on it. You must know what God's word has said.

Hell will be populated with multitudes of people who grew up in a Christian family and a Bible preaching Baptist church. Make sure that you are not one of those people. Make sure that you are real.

It is a great privilege to be in a Christian family. It is an even greater honor to be in God's family!

Endnotes

[1] Galaxie Software. (2002). 10,000 Sermon Illustrations. Biblical Studies Press.

[2] http://en.wikipedia.org/wiki/Nikita_Khrushchev

[3] See this article: https://answersingenesis.org/bible-timeline/genealogy/did-adam-and-noah-really-live-over-900-years/

[4] http://money.cnn.com/2014/08/18/pf/child-cost/

[5] See the excellent article at: https://answersingenesis.org/noahs-ark/caring-for-the-animals-on-the-ark/

[6] https://answersingenesis.org/the-flood/did-meteors-trigger-noahs-flood/

[7] http://www.accuweather.com/en/weather-news/fall-weather-brings-risk-of-de/18331198

[8] Tan, P. L. (1996). Encyclopedia of 7700 Illustrations: Signs of the Times (p. 1391). Garland, TX: Bible Communications, Inc.

[9] There is very specific language found in other Bible texts that describe sexual sins. Those words are not used here to describe the action.

[10] Genesis 10:6. "Mizraim" is the Hebrew name for Egypt.

[11] Beyer, Rick (2007). The Greatest Presidential Stories Never Told. New York City: Harper Publishing

Books By Paul Schwanke

  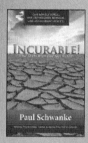 

Major Messages from Minor Prophets Series

Other Titles

Evangelist Paul Schwanke

www.preachthebible.com

Made in the USA
Lexington, KY
30 November 2019